PIONEER WOMEN

True Tales of the Old West

by

Charles L. Convis

Watercolor Cover by Mary Anne Convis

PIONEER PRESS INC., CARSON CITY, NEVADA

Library of Congress Catalog Card Number: 96-68502

ISBN 0-9651954-5-7

Printed by
KNI, Incorporated
Anaheim, California

CONTENTS

ILLUSTRATIONS

POET WITH A TEMPER

Elizabeth Winchell Markham had had enough! Their ox-drawn covered wagon had been on the trail five months since leaving Michigan. Samuel was no help. What made these fool men think that life would be better in the Oregon country, anyway? Four years before — in 1843, it was — Marcus Whitman had ridden back to the United States with his wild talk about the nation's destiny in the Northwest. Well, they'd called Michigan the Northwest when it was first settled, too. Why did men have to keep heading west, anyway? Why couldn't they be satisfied where they were?

Elizabeth loved poetry. She wrote verses from time to time, sharing them only with close, understanding friends. She liked to read other's poetry. In fact it was in Thanatopsis, written by that young boy in Massachusetts, that she first read of the Oregon — Lose thyself in the continuous woods where rolls the Oregon, and hears no sound, save its own dashings, yet the dead are there.

Well, there were dead on their trail, too. Graves all along the Platte. Some they could see from the trail, others they stumbled across while hunting buffalo chips (Elizabeth had a better word) for their cooking fires.

They had already lost three of their own, in fact. That Mr. Dunlap, who shot himself accidentally while the men looked for oxen the Indians had run off. Left a wife and six small children. Elizabeth would have liked to help, but she had all she could handle with five of her own and carrying another inside her body.

Then just a week ago, while making one of their many crossings of the Snake River, that Mister Sturges had drowned, leaving a wife and three small children, ten, four, and two. And as if that wasn't enough, the very next day two men went back to bring the rest of the cattle across. One of them, a Mister Green, slipped off his horse and sunk and was never seen again. The other man, Cornelius Smith, said all he could do was watch. Mrs. Green and six helpless children cried through that night.

Seven days after the fatal river crossing, most of the train laid by to rest. But the Markhams' company decided to move on.

Well, not Elizabeth! She knew when enough was enough. She refused to budge and she refused to let Warden, Henry and Mary go with their father and the two older boys. Samuel coaxed for three hours. Elizabeth was adamant. She was through with this Oregon foolishness!

Finally, three men in the train gently placed the younger children in their father's wagon, and it moved on ahead. Elizabeth started walking down the back trail, as the wagon hurried to make up the three hours it was behind. After she was out of sight, she took a short cut and caught up with her husband. In the meantime, Samuel had sent fifteen-year-old John back after a horse that had been left.

"Did you meet John?" Samuel asked his wife.

Elizabeth's bitterness had grown as she trudged along on her solitary walk.

"Yes," she replied, "I picked up a stone and knocked out his brains."

Samuel, shocked, left immediately to see if John was alright. Elizabeth went to one of their wagons, which contained only freight goods. She set it on fire.

When Samuel saw the flames and heard the children screaming, he ran back and put the fire out. It had burned the cover off the wagon and some of the contents. When he had finished fighting the fire, he gave Elizabeth a severe flogging.

The train had two more deaths before it reached the Oregon country. Some of the emigrants stayed at the Whitman Mission, only to be killed in the massacre a few weeks later. The Markhams went on to Oregon City.

Columbia, the Markhams' second daughter, was born in Oregon City. Elizabeth stayed with Samuel long enough to get pregnant again. Charles Edward was born in April, 1852. Shortly after that, Elizabeth and Samuel divorced.

Elizabeth opened a store in Oregon City. She published poetry in local newspapers, and was soon called the Poet Laureate of Oregon. She and the younger children moved to California when Charles was four.

Temperamental Elizabeth could not find happiness in marriage. She married and divorced again. But she must have given some of her poetic ability to her son, Charles. He took the name, Edwin, when he grew up.

Edwin's poem, *The Man with the Hoe,*" published in 1899, was called The Battle Cry of the Next Thousand Years. Translated into forty languages, it was printed in fifty thousand newspapers around the world. It brought its author a quarter of a million in royalties. Edwin Markham, whose mother wrote poetry and had a temper, was the world's greatest protagonist for social and industrial justice, the prophet for the common man. This son of Oregon's Poet Laureate became America's Poet Laureate.

Suggested reading: "The Diary of Elizabeth Dixon Smith," in Kenneth Holmes, ed. *Covered Wagon Women, v. 1,* (Glendale: The Arthur H. Clark Co., 1983).

GOODBYES TO DEAR DAUGHTERS

Tamsen Donner, five feet tall and ninety-six pounds, was all pluck. Her plain face revealed character and intelligence. She loved books, and had been happiest in school. She loved her stepmother, who had encouraged her in her studies.

Tamsen taught school in her native Massachusetts and in North Carolina. After her first husband and their two children died, Tamsen joined her brother in Illinois and continued teaching.

Tamsen particularly liked botany. While collecting samples one day, she met George Donner, who had been widowed twice and had two daughters by his second wife. Friendship soon led to marriage.

Remembering how much she loved her own stepmother, Tamsen treated George's daughters well. Soon she had three daughters of her own.

When George, sixty-two, and brother Jacob decided to emigrate to California in 1846, Tamsen, forty-five, loaded books into their wagons.

"I'll see that our girls and Jacob's children are properly educated," she vowed. "They won't go without books, even though it's a new country."

The emigrants bogged down in deep Sierra snow. The first rescue party reached them in February, 1847. George had injured his hand, and gangrene slowly spread up his arm. Jacob had already died. The rescue party could only take adults and older children who did not have to be carried. Tamsen's stepdaughters and two of Jacob's children were allowed to go. Tamsen kissed her stepdaughters goodbye, wondering if she would ever see them again.

Two weeks later the second rescue party took three more of Jacob's children. Tamsen was strong enough to go, but she refused to leave her husband and their small daughters.

Three men who came with the second rescue party stayed, saying they would care for the survivors until more help arrived. The emigrants, other than the Donners, had built shelters near Truckee Lake. The Donners were six miles below, on Alder Creek.

While one of the three men was hunting, the other two went to the Donner shelters. Tamsen agreed to pay them five hundred dollars to take her three daughters to Sutter's Fort. Frances, six, Georgia, four, and Eliza, three, said a tearful goodbye to their father. Tamsen brushed the girls' hair and dressed them in their best clothing, which she had carefully stored in their rude shelter.

"You don't want to be ragamuffins," she said. "Remember to tell people that you are the children of George Donner."

The girls nodded gravely. Georgia and Eliza wore bright red coats with matching hoods. Frances wore a cloak with a blue hood. They looked like they had stepped out of some fairy tale.

Tamsen spoke softly as she hugged her daughters. The children thought she was talking to herself. They remembered her saying something about God.

The two men took the girls to the shelters at the lake, abandoned them, and fled with the money. Now the girls had to share a strange shelter with others, including Lewis Keseberg, a frightening man who was obviously living on human flesh and enjoyed talking about it. Little Eliza began to whimper.

"Shut up, or I'll shoot you!" Keseberg shouted.

Georgia remembered that during one of the nights they shared the cabin with Keseberg, another child slept with him and was dead the next morning. Keseberg hung the dead child on a hook in the wall.

A three-day storm hit, the worst of the winter. Four days after the storm ended, Tamsen learned that her girls had been abandoned and were still at the lake shelters. She went there immediately and found them, terrified, with no hope left. She stayed overnight to protect the girls from the hateful Keseberg.

The next day a four-man relief party arrived. They said they would leave right away with the four children still alive, including Tamsen's three. They wanted Tamsen to go with them and save herself, too. George's gangrene had now reached his shoulder.

"Could I go back to see how George is?" Tamsen asked.

"It would mean a day's delay, ma'am. We can't risk it. These children need to go right now."

Tamsen bid her daughters another solemn goodbye. She turned toward her husband's shelter, six miles away. Her slow footsteps crunched in the snow. She was unable to turn her head and look back at the three little girls, standing together, their coats no longer so sparkling clean. Her shoulders shook, and she buried her face in her hands as she trudged away.

When the next rescue party came, all were dead except Lewis Keseberg. He bragged that Tamsen Donner tasted the best of all.

Suggested reading: George R. Stewart, *Ordeal by Hunger* (Boston: Houghton Mifflin Company, 1960).

CALIFORNIA SUNSHINE

Louisiana Irwin, twenty, met Dr. John Strentzel, twenty-eight, at her northeastern Texas home in 1841. John, a veteran of the Polish patriot army, had graduated from medical school in Hungary and then emigrated to the United States. He had just spent a year in his log cabin on the Trinity River, built where Dallas now stands. Louisiana shared John's love of the out-of-doors. Two years later they married. By 1849 they had two children, Louisa Wanda, three, and John, a year younger. In that year they joined a company of 135, including eight other women and twenty-three other children, traveling to California.

The Red River Company, as it came to be called, was the first group of Argonauts from northeastern Texas to go to the goldfields. They had a good wagon road to the Brazos River, crossing it after a month of travel.

A month later death made the first of its six visits to the company. A man, ailing when they started, died of liver disease. Soon after, Louisiana became sick with fever. John feared that she would die, but she recovered in two weeks.

For the next three hundred miles, the emigrants had trouble finding water. Once, when he was down to his last quart, John spoon-fed the precious liquid to his wife and children.

The Strentzels lost one team of horses in the waterless stretch. Another drowned crossing the Pecos.

"Seems like either too little water or too much," Louisiana said.

When they reached the Rio Grande, opposite the Mexican town of El Paso del Norte, some of the Argonauts gave up and returned to San Antonio. The Strentzels rested their animals, joined a re-organized group, and continued on.

The journey to the Gila River seemed like a pleasure trip. They stopped for a day or two at each Mexican village along the way.

The company found water along the Gila River, although the dust was a foot deep. They reached the Colorado River on October 15. Naturalist John J. Audubon was one day ahead of them on the trail. While waiting to cross into California, one of Strentzel's group was killed by Yuma Indians.

Strentzel was down to one wagon, a carriage, and eight mules. The hardest part of the journey, crossing the Mojave Desert, lay ahead.

Twelve days were required to cross the desert, a "wild waste of sand." "The teams would sink in almost half way to their knees

at every step," Strentzel wrote. "Our children were all day without food. Captain Pruitsfelt brought a small cake of cornbread and presented it to them. Their mother saved a bit of this bread in a small glass case as a memento of those times."

During one day's desert travel, Strentzel counted twenty-seven dead animals along the trail.

The Strentzels stayed at the mission in San Diego for six weeks. Louisiana wrote her parents:

"We know not yet whether we shall settle in California or return to Texas, it is altogether owing to how we like the country when we see more of it. The doctor has not been sick a day. I have never enjoyed better health in my life. Little Pussy and Johnny have not been sick an hour since we left Bonham."

The dark memories of Louisiana's near death along the Brazos, of spooning water into the parched throats of their children, of watching some of their horses die from lack of water and others from too much of it had already dimmed in the California sunshine.

In January, 1850, they continued north along the coast, turning inland to settle on the Tuolumne River. Strentzel set up a hotel, ferry, and store at French Bar. One of the Red River Company men, whose wife had died on the trail, settled nearby with his children. He was killed by a grizzly bear. Strentzel once had a narrow escape from three grizzlies.

For health reasons the Strentzels moved to the coast and eventually to Benicia. There, their daughter married a Scottish naturalist who shared his in-laws' love for the out-of-doors. The Strentzels gave the newly-weds the family home and built a smaller one nearby. Their son had died of diphtheria in 1857. Louisiana and John lived out their lives in the small house.

John died on Louisiana's sixty-ninth birthday. She lived seven more years. She and John had shared the philosophy of their son-in-law, Louisa's husband, John Muir:

"I went out for a walk and decided to stay until sundown, for I found that going out is really going in."

Suggested reading: Charles L. Convis, "A Journey Over the Texas-Gila River Route to the California Goldfields," in *The Far-Westerner*, v. 29 (1988).

DEATH VALLEY HEROINE

Juliet Brier, her Methodist-preacher husband, and their three small sons reached Salt Lake City late in the 1849 gold rush. With the Donner tragedy on their minds, the latecomers worried about crossing the Sierras in winter. About one hundred wagons of them, including the Briers, headed down the Old Spanish Trail toward Los Angeles. The Briers traveled with the Jayhawkers, a group of thirty-six young men from Illinois.

As they neared Mountain Meadows in southwestern Utah, some talked about striking straight west toward California's San Joaquin Valley. Reverend Brier spoke the loudest about the advantages of the short cut. Emigrants with twenty-seven wagons took his advice and turned into the unknown mountains of southern Nevada.

"You're riding straight into the jaws of hell," said the leader of the train they left. "We ain't responsible for what happens."

From time to time the split-off group met a solitary Indian. The Indians always shook their heads and pointed south toward the Old Spanish Trail.

The emigrants struggled up one dry, alkali canyon after another, seeking a way through the terrible desert. Range after range of mountains loomed up in front of them. Gradually all organization disappeared. The desperate travelers struggled forward with little communication between groups. They found water in a few small streams and seeps, but it often made them sick.

Keeping her three boys moving left Juliet no time to think about herself. For a time she had to carry little Kirke on her back. After she carried him a while, the boy would say, "Let me down, mother, I can make it now."

But the poor little fellow would stumble over the salty marsh until he sank down and could go no further. Then his mother would lift him to her back again, sometimes falling to her knees in the effort.

"The little ones would beg me piteously for a drop of water, but we had none to give them," she said later. "Many times when night came, my husband would be on ahead looking for water, and I would search on my hands and knees in the starlight for the tracks of the oxen."

As their oxen weakened, the emigrants abandoned their wagons. They killed the weakest animals, stripped the scant meat from the bones, and dried it in the smoke of their burning wagons. Instead of marrow, the bones contained only a bloody slime, but it was eaten, too.

But Juliet never gave up hope. In addition to caring for her husband and children, she gathered up oxen abandoned by other emigrants and herded the animals along.

"Who knows?" she said. "The oxen might be useful when we reach civilization."

The Jayhawkers and the Briers reached Furnace Creek in what would come to be called Death Valley on Christmas Day. The men wanted something to remind them of other days, so Reverend Brier preached a sermon on the advantages of education. William Manly, a member of another group, spent that Christmas with the Jayhawkers. He thought Brier's sermon topic odd.

One of the Jayhawkers, Doctor Fred Carr, urged Juliet to stay at Furnace Creek with her boys until a relief party could be sent back.

"I have never been a hindrance," she said. "I have never kept anyone waiting. Every step I take will be toward California." She moved on with the men.

When they crossed the 11,000-foot Panamint Range, the emigrants climbed to peaks and carried down snow for their oxen to eat. They still had three hundred miles of desert to cross in what had become a race against death.

As long as the Jayhawkers lived they talked with respect about Juliet Brier. She was always in the rear, bringing up the children and the oxen. It was she who kept the stragglers moving. Toward the end she lifted her husband to his feet every morning and held him steady until he could walk. Reverend Brier normally weighed 175, but he had lost a hundred pounds.

The desert crossing took three months. The emigrants' first fresh food was three horses they killed in early February. They found some California vaqueros who helped them reach the San Francisquito Rancho near present Newhall.

Juliet grazed her little herd of oxen until they recovered. Their sale brought enough to buy a half interest in a boarding house, which supported them until Reverend Brier could start preaching again. He preached the first protestant sermon heard in southern California.

Eventually the Briers settled in Lodi, northern California. Juliet Brier, a tough little woman, died in 1913, just four months short of her one hundredth birthday.

Suggested reading: L. Burr Belden, *Death Valley Heroine*, (San Bernardino: Inland Printing & Engraving, 1954).

TWICE A CAPTIVE

Cynthia Parker was twice captured. The first captivity brought a kind husband and wonderful children. The second brought sorrow and death.

Cynthia's preacher father, Silas, led his Baptist congregation to Texas in 1832. They settled in the Navasota River bottom, building a fort for protection from Indians. Split cedar posts, sharpened at one end and buried three feet in the ground at the other, made a secure stockade. Narrow rifle slots in the walls would allow defense against marauding Indians. Blockhouses at opposite corners had rifle slots in their overhanging floors, so savages could be shot from above. The settlers even cut down trees in the river bottom to provide a good view and a clear field of fire. But on May 19, 1836, they left the gate wide open.

The thirty-four persons living in Parker's Fort thought they would be safe. Less than a month before, Sam Houston and his rag tag band of Texians had won independence from Mexico. The Comanche, Kiowa and Caddo Indians in the area had seemed peaceful.

"Indians, Indians," someone shouted about nine o'clock that May morning. Benjamin Parker walked out the open gate, confident that the Indians were peaceful.

"Don't go, Ben," brother Silas pleaded.

"See their white flag? They only want to talk."

Ben met with the Indians and returned to the fort.

"They said they only wanted food and directions to a water hole," he announced.

"Water!" Silas shouted in derision. "They just rode across the Navasota. Their horses are dripping wet!"

"Well, to tell the truth, I am a mite worried. But I'll take them some beef and see if they're satisfied."

The Indians clubbed Ben to death and scalped him in front of his relatives and friends, including nine-year-old Cynthia.

The attack lasted a half hour. Only eighteen survived, twelve of them children. The Comanches took Cynthia and four others captive and rode away.

Comanche men considered all women as servants. They enslaved their captive women.

Sometime in the 1840s Peta Nocona, the warrior who had led the attack on Parker's Fort, took Cynthia as his wife. He treated her well, and she returned his affection.

Eventually the Comanches sold back to the whites the other persons they had captured at Parker's Fort. But they supported Cynthia in her desire to stay with the tribe, and they steadfastly refused all

offers of ransom.

Most leading Comanche warriors had two or three wives. Peta Nocona never had another. Cynthia bore him two sons, Quanah and Pecos, and a daughter, Topsannah.

In 1851 a group of traders said they saw Cynthia in a Comanche village. She was married, they said "to a great, greasy, lazy buck."

"I am happily married," Cynthia had told them. "I love my husband, who is good and kind, and my little ones, who, too, are his. I cannot forsake them."

Several times large sums of money were offered to the Comanches for Cynthia. They honored her wishes and refused to bargain.

In December 1860, Texas Rangers captured Cynthia in a running battle near the Pease River. She was clutching her baby daughter in her arms when the Rangers overpowered her. The rangers took Cynthia to an interpreter for questioning. At first she refused to talk. When assured that the whites would not harm her, she asked, "Are my sons safe?"

Twenty-five years had passed since the attack on the fort. When Parker relatives confronted Cynthia, they saw only a hostile Comanche woman before them. Nothing reminded them of the nine-year-old girl they had once known.

Sul Ross, leader of the rangers in the Pease River battle, came home a hero and became governor of Texas. Cynthia knew that the great disaster of her life was not being captured and raised by the Comanches. It was being torn away from the husband she loved and the children she cherished.

The efforts of family and neighbors to help Cynthia adjust to white society only strengthened her desire to return to her true home. An uncle took her to Fort Worth and gave her a fine cabin of her own. They had to lock her in at night.

Neighbors often saw her during the day as she sat on the front porch, her baby at her breast, tears streaming down her face. Cynthia's brother, who had been captured in the same raid and later escaped, took her to live with his family. She never stopped grieving the loss of her husband and sons.

Topsannah died at five. Cynthia buried the girl in a white graveyard. In 1870, her heart still broken, Cynthia ended her second captivity by starving herself to death.

Suggested reading: Margaret S. Hacker, *Cynthia Ann Parker* (El Paso: Texas Western Press, 1994).

MATHILDA FRIEND, A FIGHTER

The darkest days in Legion Valley history were February 5 and 6, 1867. The pretty valley, sixteen miles south of Llano, Texas, had heavy rain on the fourth, turning to snow on the fifth. Visitors at the John Friend cabin wondered how they would get home in the snow and bitter cold.

"Oh pshaw," nineteen-year-old Mathilda Friend said. "You can't go out in this weather with them babies. We can make room here for everybody."

"Everybody" included — besides Mathilda — her husband and his eight-year-old son, Lee, the Boyd Johnson and Frank Johnson families, nineteen-year-old Amanda Townsend, and eleven-year-old Malenda Caudle.

The next day John Friend and the Johnson brothers went to town for lumber. They did not expect hostile Indians, as none had been seen for several weeks.

"You men just go on," Mathilda said. "We'll be fine. Give us a chance to visit over our hand work."

That afternoon the Caudle girl and Lee Friend ran inside from their play in the snow, screaming "Indians." Each Johnson woman had an infant girl. They and Amanda became even more afraid than the children.

"What will we do?" they wailed. "They'll kill us sure."

Mathilda bolted the cabin door. While the other women screamed in fright, she ran to lock the rear window.

Twenty-two Comanches crashed through the door. Mathilda grabbed a rifle and was raising it to shoot when an arrow struck her arm. One Indian wrenched her rifle away as others broke through the window.

She seized a flat iron and knocked the closest Indian down. The Indian holding her rifle, seeing his comrade fall, raised the weapon to shoot, but Mathilda grabbed a chair and knocked him down.

Another Indian shot an arrow into her chest. She grabbed a knife from the table as she fell to the floor. An Indian wrenched the knife away, almost severing her fingers. She passed out as he scalped her.

The Indians looted the cabin and bound their seven captives. Before riding away, one of them came back to see if Mathilda was really dead. She had recovered enough to see him coming. She lay still in spite of the excruciating pain when he hacked her arms to the bone and jerked on the arrow in her chest.

Mathilda crawled to the Jack Bradford cabin, a mile and a half away. She had to stop often for rest. She bathed her bloody face and arm with snow, and she packed snow against the terrible wound where her scalp had been ripped away.

She collapsed, exhausted, at Bradford's door but was able to tell what had happened. She begged Bradford to pull the arrow out of her chest. He tried, unsuccessfully.

Bradford carried her inside, worried that the Indians would follow her trail of blood to his cabin. He bandaged her wounds, threw more wood on the fire, and put a bucket of water by her as she lay on the floor.

"You'll be warm and there's water to drink," he said. "I have to hide my family in the cedar break. I hope you understand."

When news of the attack reached Llano, every able bodied man rode out at once. Doctor Hardin Oatman treated Mathilda's wounds. Other men followed the Indians' trail, then thirty-six hours old.

The next morning, about five miles from the Friend cabin, they found both Johnson babies. One had been brained against a tree, the other's throat was slashed from ear to ear. They found the bodies of the Johnson women and Amanda Townsend. All had been stripped, mutilated and scalped.

Three years later Malenda Caudle, who had been recovered by army troops, filled in some details.

The raiding party had included two or three women, one of whom protected Malenda and treated her as an adopted daughter. Just before the first evening camp, one of the babies had cried loudly for its mother. The warrior holding the baby choked it into silence. The mother, riding behind the warrior, tried to take her baby away. The warrior got mad and slammed the baby against a tree. That night the victorious warriors raped the three women over and over again.

The next morning a warrior cut the throat of the other baby, holding it head down in front of its mother so she could see the blood pouring into the snow. The warriors laughed as the mother screamed and fainted. Then they killed the two Johnson women and Amanda Townsend.

Three weeks after the attack, Mathilda Friend gave birth to a healthy baby daughter. Mathilda's head was still so swollen from her scalping that she could not see her new baby until it was seven weeks old.

Suggested reading: Wilburn Oatman, *Llano, Gem of the Hill Country* (Hereford, Texas: Pioneer Book Publ., 1970).

INDIAN CAPTIVES

Sarah White, seventeen, was living on a farm in the Republican River bottom of Cloud County, Kansas, in 1868. On August 13, while hoeing in the garden, she looked up to see four Cheyenne warriors enter the house.

"Indians," Sarah shouted to her father, working in a nearby field. She started toward the house, fearing for her mother and the smaller children.

But some Indians ran to her father and killed him. Others caught Sarah and dragged her away. They bound her, threw her across a horse, and fled toward their village, far to the south.

Two months later, in neighboring Ottawa County, Anna Brewster Morgan was celebrating her first month's wedding anniversary. She had been living in the Solomon River bottom with her brother, David Brewster. Anna and David were orphans. Their father had been killed in the Civil War, and their mother had died in an insane asylum. Anna had fallen in love with neighbor James Morgan and had moved to his homestead just one month before.

Raiding Sioux swooped down to wound James and capture Anna. The Indian marauders rode south across the Arkansas River, where they traded Anna to the same band of Cheyennes which had captured Sarah.

Indian raids along the Republican, Solomon, and Saline Rivers that summer had the Kansas frontier in a turmoil. After the capture of Sarah and Anna, the legislature authorized the formation of a volunteer regiment of Kansas Cavalry. Within three weeks the regiment was at full strength. Governor Samuel Crawford resigned his office to take command.

The 7th United States Cavalry under George Custer had just destroyed a Cheyenne village on the Washita River in Indian Territory. The new Kansas Volunteer regiment joined Custer's troops at Camp Supply and awaited orders from General Philip Sheridan.

In the meantime David Brewster left his homestead to ride to Camp Supply. There he persuaded Custer to let him ride with the cavalry and help search for the Indians who held his sister captive.

"Her husband is still recovering from his wounds, colonel," David said. "He'll be crippled for life. My sister needs me to help find her."

"You're welcome to ride with the regiment. We'll do our best to find her."

Sheridan ordered the troops out on December 7 to search for the Sioux, Cheyenne, and Kiowa bands, which had been raiding whites. The cavalry lost so many horses in the bitter cold that Sheridan, taking personal command, demobilized the volunteer regiment and gave their horses to Custer's regiment. Brewster stayed on with the continuing expedition.

In the meantime Anna and Sarah slipped away from the Indians in the deep snow and headed north. But the Cheyennes recaptured them, punished them viciously, and took them back to the Indian village. Sarah almost lost her feet to frostbite.

On March 22, 1869, Custer's cavalry found the Cheyenne band which had the two women. They were in Wheeler County, Texas, about eighty miles west of the site of the Washita Battle.

Custer smoked the peace pipe with the Cheyennes and accepted their offer to send chiefs and warriors to the cavalry camp for an evening of music and dancing. During the evening's performance, soldiers suddenly overpowered the four chiefs who came. They released one to carry this message:

"We'll hold the other three until you bring the women in, safe from harm."

After more negotiations, Custer sent another message:

"If the women aren't here by sundown, Dull Knife, Big Head, and Fat Bear will be executed. The firing squad is ready."

The sun was low in the sky when the Indians brought in Sarah and Anna. Custer described his soldiers' reaction to the recovery of the captives:

"Men whom I have seen face death without quailing found their eyes filled with tears, unable to restrain the deep emotion produced by this joyful event."

Anna Morgan was a strikingly beautiful woman. She had blue eyes, a lovely complexion, and lustrous, blonde hair. A few months after her recapture, she had a half-Indian child, which died two years later.

Anna rejoined her husband after he got out of the hospital. They had three children, but her husband left her, and she and the children went to live with her brother, David. She died, insane, in the Topeka Hospital for the Feeble Minded.

Sarah White married a Civil War veteran. They had seven children. She lived to be eighty-nine. She spent her last years with a son, a few miles from the place where she had been captured. She seldom spoke about her captivity or treatment.

Suggested reading: George A. Custer, *My Life on the Plains* (Lincoln, Univ. of Nebraska Press, 1966).

AN INDEPENDENT WOMAN

Mary Richardson, farm girl in Maine, wanted to serve God in foreign missions. But missionaries had to be married, and Mary had no husband. She had a proposal from a well-to-do neighbor, but she was not sure money made up for meager education and lack of refinement.

Mary asked her diary: Shall I escape the horrors of perpetual celibacy and settle down with the vulgar?

Her answer — No!

Then she met Elkanah Walker, six feet, four inches tall, ungainly, and too shy to speak easily with strangers. Mary, unimpressed at first, learned that Elkanah wanted to be a missionary, too. Aha! Mary's mind began working.

Ten months later, in March 1838, Mary, twenty-six, married Elkanah, thirty-three. They left the next day for the Northwest. Mary wore black to symbolize her grief at parting forever from her family.

Mary was one month pregnant when their wagon train pulled out of Westport, Missouri, in late April. She and Elkanah would have to ride horseback almost two thousand miles.

In June Mary told her diary: I regard my husband as a special blessing conferred by Heaven, and I am determined if possible that my life shall evince my gratitude.

Two weeks later: I think I am rather happy.

They reached the Oregon country in late August. Too late in the year to build their own cabin, they spent the winter in the Marcus Whitman quarters, sharing the cramped space with seven adults and two children.

Cyrus was born on December 7. After five hours of labor, during which she almost wished she had never married, Mary heard the baby cry.

She told her diary: Soon I forgot my misery in the joy of possessing a proper child. I truly felt to say with Eve, I have gotten a man from the Lord.

By April, Elkanah and Mary and another couple had started their own mission, but Mary began to question her commitment to missionary work.

"I seem to be more interested in the natural sciences than learning the Indians' language," she told Elkanah.

"You should not spend the sabbath reading books unless they're about religion," her husband advised.

Mary berated herself for not matching Elkanah's commitment. But her self-inflicted guilt never overcame her

independence. When Elkanah criticized her for reading botany books, she just read more botany and felt more guilt.

Mary had collected plants on her trip west. When German botanist Karl Geyer stopped at the mission on his scientific expedition, Mary's collection grew rapidly. The botanist expressed high praise for Mary's scientific attitude and her hospitality.

Mary was also interested in taxidermy. She mounted a large collection of birds and animals.

Nine years after Mary and Elkanah reached the Oregon country, Cayuse Indians killed Marcus and Narcissa Whitman and eight other persons at the Whitman Mission. Mary wrote: May God have compassion on those that survive and stay the hand of the ruthless savages.

After the Whitman massacre, the church ordered the Walkers' mission closed. Mary and Elkanah moved to the Willamette Valley in Oregon.

These two independent people, who learned to love each other while raising their eight children, finally parted in November, 1877.

On his death bed Elkanah asked Mary if she would promise to not remarry. The 65-year-old faithful wife, who had no intention of ever marrying again, refused to make the promise.

A month after Elkanah died, Mary wrote:

> And now I recollect with pain
> The many times I grieved him sore
> Oh, if he would but come again
> I think I'd vex him so no more.

After Elkanah died Mary's mind began to slip. She had kept the sidesaddle she had ridden across the plains and mountains so many years before. She enjoyed strapping the saddle to a bench and sitting in it with her old cape thrown across her shoulders. With her eyes half closed and her head held high, she relived the memories of learning to love the man she had married.

Mary lived another twenty years, dying at eighty-five, still unmarried. Six of her children plus twenty-five grandchildren and six great-grandchildren survived her.

Two of her granddaughters had their grandmother's love for science. They both earned doctorates and became professors of botany at the University of Nebraska.

Suggested reading: Clifford Drury, Elkanah and Mary Walker (Caldwell: Caxton Printers, 1940).

MARY RICHARDSON WALKER

Oregon Historical Society, Neg. No. CN 017573

EILLEY ORRUM BOWERS

Nevada Historical Society

QUEEN OF WASHOE

The blood of Scottish kings coursed through fifteen-year-old Eilley Orrum's veins, but her household tasks seemed harsh and endless. When she peered out the small window of the hut where her impoverished parents were raising too many children, she could see the old castle on the hill.

What would it be like to live in such a grand castle? she wondered.

Eilley's only escape came from reading her fortune in daisy petals, in swirling clouds, in evening stars. Sister Betsy and her husband, Jim, had abandoned their Presbyterian faith to become Mormons. They were packing to join a colony in Nauvoo, Illinois, in far-off America.

"Take me with you," Eilley pleaded. "I'll be a Mormon, too."

Betsy looked at her sister's work-heavy stoop, her water-bleached hands. "Of course you may come with us."

The Mormons were delighted with the healthy, buxom girl as a new convert. At Nauvoo she married Elder Hunter, three times her age. He had just buried his wife.

Hunter, a kind man, soon became a bishop. He and Eilley moved to the new colony Brigham Young was building beside Great Salt Lake. As Hunter's prestige and responsibilities increased, he brought home three more women, one at a time. He introduced them to a perplexed Eilley as additional wives. Eilley, unwilling to share her only chance to get ahead in the world, got a divorce.

Eilley took another Mormon husband, Alex Cowan, who had no other marital obligations. In 1854 Eilley persuaded him to move to the Washoe country, far to the west. She thought their chance to get ahead would be better there.

Alex wanted to farm in the new country.

"It's better to prospect for gold," Eilley insisted. "I'll help out by running a boarding house for other prospectors."

In 1857 Brigham Young called back the faithful to defend Zion against the United States Army. Eilley, unhappy with Alex's meager efforts at prospecting, saw a way to get another divorce. She refused to go back to Zion.

One day a boarder gave Eilley a ten foot claim to pay his bill. It adjoined the claim of another boarder, Sandy Bowers. Bowers, a mule skinner from Missouri, had driven an emigrant's wagon west. He could not read, but he worked hard. Eilley married him.

In a few years their Imperial mine, developed from the two ten-foot claims, was producing a million dollars a year. Eilley now told her fortune with a crystal ball. She saw herself as a queen, earning respectful salutes from the miners around her.

"I'll build myself a real castle," Eilley vowed.

She brought an architect from San Francisco and stonecutters from Scotland. She built her mansion in Washoe Valley, where the land — except for the magnificent Sierra backdrop — resembled her native Scotland.

But the money came too fast to spend in castle building. Eilley and Sandy went to Europe in 1861 to buy furnishings fit for the best home between the Mississippi River and the West Coast. They bought furniture carved in Belgium and a pair of three-thousand-dollar mirrors from a Venetian palace. They bought dozens of sets of morocco-bound books with their name, which Sandy could not read, engraved in gold letters. They shipped bullion from their mine to Europe to be cast into a special table service.

Eilley's only disappointment was not being received by Queen Victoria. The queen did not receive divorced women. But Eilley, still a subject of her majesty, did bring ivy from Windsor Castle to plant by her castle in America.

Silver from the Imperial mine was a major source of financing for the Union cause in the Civil War. But when the war ended, production declined. Eilley paid little attention. When Sandy died in 1868, a shocked Eilley learned that his entire estate was appraised at $638,000. The house, alone, had cost a half million! What had happened to the mine? A stunned Eilley did not understand that all the Comstock mines were declining rapidly.

Eilley knew what to do! She went back to the rooming and boarding business. She added a third floor of guest rooms to her castle. She built bath houses by the swimming pool. She hired a hundred security officers for opening day. But the business did not last. Within a year Eilley lost the home to creditors.

Eilley moved to Virginia City to tell fortunes. Then, penniless, she wandered on to Reno and then to San Francisco. Her fortune-telling income and handouts from friends kept her alive until 1903.

Friends buried her next to Sandy behind her castle in Washoe Valley.

Suggested reading: Alice B. Addenbrooke, *The Mistress of the Mansion* (Palo Alto: Pacific Books, 1950).

GOLIGHTLY'S OTHER WIFE

Residents of Salt Lake City in the 1850s loved an old Scotsman, affectionately called Golightly. A baker by trade, a musician by nature, and a good Mormon by practice, he had many customers who savored his bread, biscuits and cakes.

Golightly's spiritual wife lived in a little house at the side of the bakery shop. People wondered about an old woman who slept in a wagon behind the shop with three daughters, thirteen, fifteen, and seventeen, and an eleven-year-old son.

The daughters would help Golightly bake, as their mother sat close to the fireplace, seldom speaking. Sometimes Golightly's spiritual wife came to the shop, but none ever saw her and the old woman together. The old woman seemed in poor health. She usually sat in a morose silence, a blanket drawn tightly around her.

One day Golightly was away when Solomon Carvalho, artist and roving reporter, dropped by for his daily dessert. Then Carvalho learned the old woman's story.

"Golightly and I were happy in Edinburgh," she told Carvalho. "In twenty-five years I bore the mon twelve bairnies. Only four were alive when the Mormon missionaries came. We had a prosperous bakery trade, a comfortable home, and owed not a cent. But Golightly got baptized, and nothing would do but he had to go to America and live in the new Zion.

"He even tried to convert me. I was raised Presbyterian, and I dinna want America or Zion or nae part of it. He sold everything, left us with a pittance, and sailed away with the ither converts."

Golightly wrote back from Salt Lake City that he had built a small house by his bakery shop, and he implored his wife and family to join him. The old woman decided to face the dangers of an ocean voyage and brave the perils of crossing the plains and mountains to be with the old man she had loved so long. With the help of friends, she converted her small property to money. She had two hundred English pounds for the journey.

After a terrible time with sea sickness, she and her children reached New York, where she bought "through tickets" to Salt Lake City. The agent was a cheat, and but for the kindness of the conductor, who allowed them to go to St. Louis, they would have been stranded.

Somehow they reached Independence, where the old woman spent the last of her money on a team and wagon. When they reached Fort Laramie, she inquired of eastbound travelers from Salt Lake City if they knew Golightly.

"A stranger told me Golightly and his wife were both well

and living very comfortably," she continued with Carvalho.

"I said, surely mon, you mak a mistake. Golightly has nae ither wife but me.'

"But they insisted he had taken a spiritual wife.

"'A spiritual wife,' said I. 'I dinna ken the kind.'"

Thinking the travelers were mistaken and that her husband had hired a servant girl, she traveled on. But the awful truth sunk in when she reached Salt Lake City and learned of Mormon polygamy. Poor in health from the long journey, she fell in a swoon when she learned of the horrible repudiation from the man to whom she had given her life.

Golightly tried to carry her into his house. She roused enough to say, "My foot shall niver cross the threshold of a house that contains anither wife. This wagon shall be my house and my children's house. During the howlings of the winter's blast or the scorching heat of the summer, I will abide, until death takes me away."

She did relent enough to eventually come into the shop, where she watched glumly as the husband of her youth worked with their children. The spiritual wife knew better than to come out at those times. The old woman finally agreed to be baptized, just to please the old man whom she still loved. After being immersed on a bitter cold day, she said it did no good.

"I canna see ony different now. I am only the worse in the body."

The old woman leaned closer to Carvalho. "And who do ye think he married?" she asked. "Surely nabodie but our auld cook from Edinburgh, a dirty wench that I turned out of me house for impertinence. She followed the old man and induced him to marry her, telling him I niver intended to come out to him. I niver set eyes on her here, and she takes good care to niver come where I am."

"Aye, it's a true story," Golightly told Carvalho. "But she should ken, I still love her. I sent for her and took good care of her. I took the spiritual wife only for the other woman's eternal salvation."

Suggested reading: S. N. Carvalho, *Incidents of Travel and Adventure in the Far West* (Philadelphia: Jewish Pub. Soc., 1954).

WILL OF THE WISP

We don't know her name, but she flitted from man to man during her short appearance in the West, bringing tragedy to almost everything she touched.

As the curtain rises in our western melodrama, she is married to one Carter, a down-on-his-luck miner at Virginia City, Nevada. Henry Comstock was superintendent of the Ophir Mine when Carter asked for work. Comstock stared at Carter's dilapidated wagon. The man's only home, it contained all his worldly possessions.

"You living in that wagon?" Comstock asked.

"It's all we got — me and the woman. I need work bad. We come from Salt Lake."

Comstock's gaze shifted from the small, insignificant man to his wife, and his brain whirled. The young beauty's dark eyes gazed mournfully from beneath her calico sunbonnet. They pleaded for adventure. Comstock, like David upon seeing Bathsheba, was smitten immediately. And like David, Comstock was not slow at intrigue. He hired Carter, sent him to a distant work place, and turned his attention to the wagon and its beautiful inhabitant.

After a quick marriage in Washoe Valley, the newlyweds went to Carson City. There, while Comstock's friends congratulated the beaming groom, Carter showed up and demanded his wife back.

Comstock knew that Carter, a Mormon, had probably married without a license.

"Here's my paper," Comstock sneered. "Where's yours?"

Carter walked away, dejected.

"Wait a minute," Comstock shouted. "I'll pay for her so you won't bother me no more."

Carter accepted a horse, a revolver, and sixty dollars.

"I want a regular bill of sale," Comstock demanded.

Carter signed a bill of sale, and went back to his lonely wagon with his new treasures.

With business in San Francisco, Comstock left his new bride in Carson City and started over the mountains.

"You'll be alright here," he said, kissing her goodbye. "I'll be back soon, and we'll finish the honeymoon."

When Comstock reached Sacramento, he learned that his wife had run away with a Carson City youth, heading for California by the same route Comstock had taken. He returned to Hangtown and intercepted the runaways. He took his wife to a hotel room for a long talk,

"It's all settled now," Comstock said, rejoining his friends. "She's sorry for what she did. There'll be no more trouble. She promised to be a good wife."

His Hangtown friends congratulated him.

"Let's go down to the hotel and you can all meet her," Comstock said proudly.

The hotel room was empty! The will of the wisp had climbed out a back window to rejoin her young lover. The twice-rejected husband ran to the livery barn.

"I'll pay a hundred-dollars for bringing them in," he announced. "We got plenty of horses here."

Most of the men who accepted horses smiled and went for pleasure rides. They had no intention of disturbing the young lovers. One, however, meant business. He marched the runaways back to Hangtown in front of his revolver.

Comstock paid the reward and locked his wife up. Some friends put the young wife-stealer in a room under guard. After dark the guard spoke to him.

"They done decided what to do with you. They don't call this place Hangtown fer nothin'. You'll be dancin' on air when the sun comes up yonder."

A short time later the guard opened the door again.

"I'm goin' out fer a drink. If'n yer here when I git back, you know what'll happen at sunup."

He left the door ajar, and the nervous young man was never seen again.

By watching carefully, Comstock kept his wife all winter. But when spring returned and the flowers bloomed and the sap rose again in the trees, she ran away with a man she saw strolling through the mines, his blankets on his back. Apparently tired of drifting with the tides, we are told she dropped anchor in a Sacramento saloon.

Comstock went broke, drifted to the Montana gold fields, and killed himself with a shot to the head.

Carter, who may or may not have been the Will of the Wisp's first man, also had a tragic fate. He used the horse and money Comstock gave him to go to California. Within a week he had married a young emigrant girl. They returned to Virginia City, where the bride learned about her husband selling her predecessor. She got a divorce and married a Mr. Winnie of nearby Gold Hill.

Winnie and Carter had frequent arguments which ended when Winnie shot Carter to death.

Like a barroom melodrama, the tragedy continued. Winnie moved to Honey Lake Valley, where his young wife was thrown from a horse and killed.

Suggested reading: Dan De Quille, *History of the Big Bonanza* (Hartford, American Publishing Co., 1877).

SAFE UNDER THE SHADOW OF HIS WING

Eighteen-year-old Esther McMillan had been Mrs. Joseph Hanna for one hour when they boarded the steamship in Pittsburgh. It was March 11, 1852, and Joseph, a brand new Presbyterian minister, was leaving the country to carry the Word of God to the Oregon wilderness. They stayed over for the Sabbath in Cincinnati. The newly-weds heard one minister preach in the morning, another in the evening.

The smelly, overcrowded boat that carried them on to St. Louis annoyed Esther. Their two-day stay in St. Louis included the Sabbath. Again they observed it properly by worshipping, not working or traveling.

But young Esther loved the world, too. That St. Louis morning, as church bells chimed, she jerked the pillow away from sleeping Joseph. Then she folded her hands primly like an old married woman when her astonished husband sat up in bed.

"Good morning your worship," she said with mock seriousness. Glad to reach St. Louis after the dangerous boat trip, Esther wrote that evening in her diary: Oh, may I at all times trust in the Lord and feel safe under the shadow of His wing.

They waited five weeks in St. Joseph, Missouri, for other Presbyterians to arrive. During their wait Esther visited the local cemetery for the burial of an emigrant. That evening she wrote: I, too, am a wanderer, a pilgrim, and little know how soon my frail body will be laid by the wayside!

The group of sixty Presbyterians in eighteen wagons started west on May 4. Esther and Joseph had an ox-drawn wagon, a mule-drawn carriage, and spare mules to ride.

On May 30, four days past Fort Kearney, the caravan split up. It was Sunday, but eleven wagons of people wanted to keep traveling. The Hanna wagon stayed behind. That evening, watching the full moon and thinking of loved ones left at home, Esther broke down and cried.

A week later Esther first mentioned the choking dust. Once she was unable to see her own wagon as she walked alongside.

Two days west of Fort Laramie, they passed the grave of a man who had been murdered the day before. Later the same day, they passed the grave of his killer, already hanged.

June 27 was the first time they traveled on Sunday. Three days later Esther and Joseph had only two yoke of oxen left. They cut their wagon down to a two-wheeled cart.

By Sunday, July 4, the entire caravan had only five wagons left. The stench of dead animals along the trail sickened the travelers. They respected that Sabbath by not traveling, but they were too tired for preaching.

Esther stayed in good spirits. When they reached Soda Springs in Bear River Valley, she mixed soda-filled river water with sugar and tartaric acid from her meager stores.

"It's an excellent drink and foams nicely," she said.

As they neared Fort Hall, Esther thought of the Whitmans, massacred five years before.

She wrote: God grant that we may not share the same fate in the wilderness. We are so young and so full of the Word.

Esther liked the Shoshoni Indians better than the Sioux and Pawnees they had met east of the Rockies. The Shoshonis were more decently clothed.

By late July the daytime temperatures were up to 106 degrees, and the dust was worse. Even the animals coughed at every step.

On Sunday, July 24, they got up at three and were on the trail before daylight. A week later, their best ox died and they had to abandon the cart. They put their last yoke of oxen on another's wagon. They still had their carriage and the riding mules.

On August 6 Esther described the trail as Dante's Inferno — a barren lava waste populated with dead animals. Esther's spirits finally faltered. The caravan was down to two wagons and the Hanna carriage. She wrote: If only Mister Hanna and I would have more time together.

The next Sunday Joseph was again too tired to conduct services.

Her first view of Mt. Hood thrilled Esther. She called it "a golden cloud in the distance." They met friendly Nez Perce Indians. The Indian women had berries and fruit to trade. The white women squatted among them, chattering like magpies.

The Hannas abandoned their carriage, packed their belongings on their mules and trudged on. Joseph insisted that Esther ride a mule. She found it better than walking, but the mule laid down and died.

The next day, six months after leaving their home, they reached the Columbia River Valley. Esther thanked the Lord for leading them through to safety.

Suggested reading: Eleanor Allen, *Canvas Caravans* (Portland: Binfords & Mort, 1946).

ABIGAIL DUNIWAY MILLINERY

28

JOURNEY TO OREGON

The Tucker Scott family of Groveland, Illinois, left St. Joseph on May 10, six days behind Esther Hanna's train. By the time the Scotts reached the graves of the murdered man and his killer, they were just one day behind. The Scotts went on to Oregon, but we cannot tell if they passed the Hanna train.

Tucker Scott and his wife, Ann, had nine children. Tucker assigned duties to all but five-year-old Maria and three-year-old Willy. Seventeen-year-old Jenny (Abigail) kept the journal.

Ann Scott and her six daughters had spent all the previous winter making bedding and clothing. Tucker did not want his family to be destitute if they failed to reach Oregon in this journey of no return. Many tears were shed as the five wagons, pulled by thirty-two oxen, started west on April 2.

Six days later Mother Ann was so sick she could not travel, and they laid over three days until she improved. Passing through Missouri, where she saw slaves working in fields, depressed Jennie even more than the sorrow of leaving home.

When they reached St. Joseph, the Scotts picked up provisions which they had shipped ahead by boat. They also joined other wagons from Illinois, making up a train of fifty-two persons, traveling in twelve wagons, with 113 oxen and twelve horses. Jenny and nineteen-year-old Mary, the family cook, took a spy glass and climbed a hill outside St. Joseph for a last, sad look at the United States.

Four days later Jenny mentioned passing seven new graves. She said the mid-May weather was cold enough for "a drear November morning."

They continued to see new graves practically every day. When they reached Fort Kearney on May 29, they were three days behind the Hanna train. At this stage, the Hannas had not traveled on Sunday; the Scotts usually did.

Two days later the Scotts met a company from Illinois which had given up to return to the states. They moved on, passing four new graves, two of which had been made by the returning train.

They killed their first buffalo on June 3. They saw four new graves on the fifth, six on the sixth. On June 7 a California-bound train, camped next to them, buried one of their members. One of the Scott train men joined the California train to replace the man who died.

During the next five days they passed twenty-nine new graves. They laid over on Sunday, June 13, to rest their oxen. Over a hundred wagons passed them as they rested.

By June 15 they could see Scott's Bluff. Sometimes they were passing ten new graves in a day. Jenny and her mother were sick with cholera, and sister Mag helped keep the journal. Jennie resumed the journal on June 20 with the sad news that her mother had died. Another woman in a nearby train also died that day. That train moved on with no delay, but the Scotts laid over a day for the burial.

The travelers wrapped Ann Scott, forty, in a feather-bed coffin. They piled rocks over the grave to protect it from wolves, and covered the rock mound with freshly-picked wild roses. None of the Scott family ever found the grave again.

They reached Independence Rock on June 29. Jennie and three of her sisters tried to climb it, but a high wind and hail stopped them. They camped that night by Devils's Gate, five miles west. The next day they passed the graves of the murdered man and his killer. Jennie identified the victim as Charles Botsford, his murderer as Horace Dolley.

On July 15 they laid over a day at the request of a nearby train from Wisconsin. A murder had been committed in that train, and the Wisconsin men asked the Illinois men to serve on a jury. The verdict was self defense.

On July 31, in crossing the Snake River, the Scotts lost three oxen and a horse. A young man in a nearby train drowned in the crossing.

Jennie complained of heat and dust in traveling along the Snake, as Esther Hanna had. In late August cholera re-appeared. Tucker Scott was quite sick — unable to walk for two days — but recovered. But Willy Scott, barely four, died on August 27. Jennie wrote that he was "called from earth to vie with angels around the throne of God." Three days later one of the men who had joined them in St. Joseph also died.

On September 8 they had their first view of Mt. Hood and Mt. St. Helens. The sight did not impress Jennie as it had Esther Hanna. Perhaps it was a dull day. Relatives who had emigrated to Oregon earlier met them as they traveled down the Columbia River Valley. They reached the end of the trail at Oregon City on September 29.

Jennie used her correct name, Abigail, when she started teaching school. Then she married Ben Duniway, a farmer. He lost the farm when he signed a promissory note for a friend. They moved to town, where a runaway accident crippled Ben. Abigail went back to teaching school.

By then Abigail and Ben had five sons and a daughter. She had to get up at three in summer and four in winter in order to prepare breakfast for the family and boarders, do the cleaning, and get to school on time. She could rest at her desk while teaching the primary classes, but she never found time to prepare for the higher grades. She worked those lessons out while her students were doing them.

Abigail had no complaints, but she thought often about the role of women in society. She remembered her mother saying, after giving birth to a daughter: "Poor baby, she'll grow up to be a woman some day." And she never got over the blow to her pride at ten when her mother told her how disappointed she was at the birth of a second daughter.

As soon as Abigail saved thirty dollars from teaching, she borrowed twelve hundred dollars to enter the millinery business. She paid the money off in three weeks.

Abigail had more time, as a businesswoman, to think about women's roles. She often remarked: "Half of us are dolls, half are drudges, and all are fools."

In 1871, 36-year-old Abigail Duniway moved her family to Portland, where she started a newspaper for women. That year she toured Oregon and Washington with Susan B. Anthony, who spoke on woman suffrage.

Perhaps remembering her own feelings as a child, Abigail was always closest to Clara, the only daughter of her six children. Heartbroken when Clara died in 1886, Abigail said, "Then I, too, wished to die. But Clara told me, 'You must stay and finish your work, ma.'"

Abigail Duniway was one of the most reviled women in the west during the early years of her campaign for women suffrage. Once, when she was riding a stage filled with men, one of them said, "Madame! you ought to be at home enjoying yourself like my wife is doing. I want to bear all the hardships myself, and let her sit by the fire, toasting her footsies."

Abigail said nothing as the other passengers poked elbows into ribs at her expense. But when the stage dropped the man in front of his rural home, everyone saw his wife outside, chopping at the woodpile.

"Good-bye," Abigail called cheerily, leaning out of the stage. "I see that your wife is toasting her footsies."

In 1912, when Abigail was seventy-seven, she signed the Oregon Proclamation giving women the vote. She lived three more years, years of honor and recognition from both women and men in her home state.

Suggested reading: Kenneth L. Holmes and David C. Duniway, *Covered Wagon Women, v. 5* (Glendale: Arthur H. Clark Co., 1986).

A GOOD FAMILY

Lura Homsley was born in Missouri in spring 1849. Her father thought it was May, but Lura never knew what day to celebrate. The family crossed the plains to Oregon in 1852. Their wagon capsized as they forded a river, and they lost the family bible containing Lura's birthdate.

Shortly before they started west, the family had included five children. Winnie, a slave girl owned by Lura's uncle, did the housework. Lura's mother liked Winnie, but Lura's father did not. His contempt for the girl was so obvious and intense that she resolved to get even.

One day, as the Homsleys prepared for their journey to Oregon, they went to town with the three youngest children, leaving Winnie to care for the oldest two. That day Winnie got even with Lura's father. She gave poison to the two children in her care, killing them both.

"Hang her," demanded some of the family.

"It would be foolish," the uncle said. "The girl is young, strong, and good-looking. Hanging her would cost me my investment."

He shipped Winnie down the Mississippi River to a slave-dealer in New Orleans.

The Homsleys began their long journey with two ox-drawn wagons. Near Fort Laramie the mother and the youngest child died of measles. Lura's father buried them at the side of the trail. The grief-stricken man scratched deeply with his jackknife into a sandstone rock to write: Mary E. Homsley, died June 10, 1852, aged 29.

When the family reached Oregon, Homsley took up a donation land claim and put his remaining two children in school. He lived to be ninety-four.

In 1864 fifteen-year-old Lura was sitting on the front porch of the home where she and sister Sarah boarded, when two young soldiers in uniform stopped to ask directions.

"My name's George Gibson," one of them said. "I'm stationed at Fort Vancouver. I'm looking for my uncle who lives around here someplace."

Lura's landlady came out as George repeated the uncle's name.

"Why he's my nearest neighbor," she said. "You boys come up and set a minute while I fetch a glass of water and show you where his cabin is."

George and his friend, Sam Taylor, were on a short furlough.

Lura's landlady could recognize an opportunity. She offered Gibson and Taylor tickets to a dance.

"Much obliged, ma'am," George said, "but we don't know any girls to take." He looked at Lura, who looked down quickly.

"That's surely no problem. You can take the Holmsley girls who live here with me." She beamed.

Within a few months the soldiers returned on another furlough, calling again on the girls.

"This was during the Civil War," Lura said when interviewed in 1932. "This young chap had on a blue uniform with brass buttons, and you know how girls fall for a uniform. You know how it is in war time. A soldier never knows where he's going to be sent next, so George suggested we get married."

George's approach worked, as it did and would for countless servicemen before and since. He and Lura married in December of that year, as did Sarah and Taylor.

When George was mustered out of the army, he and Lura lived with her father for a time. Then, with her father's help, they started a farm of their own.

Lura's family had lost all track of the trailside grave of Lura's mother and the baby. But in 1921, sixty-nine years after they died, a University of Wyoming history professor wrote Lura that the grave had been found and marked with an historical monument.

Five hundred people were present when the Wyoming Historical Society dedicated the flower-banked grave. The mayor of Laramie, Wyoming, led the ceremony. Lura was invited, but she could not attend.

Lura, eighty-three when interviewed, had ten grandchildren and ten great-grandchildren.

"Most of my girlhood friends have, by now, taken the one-way trail," she said. "I guess my time will be up soon. But I can't complain — had a good family and saw a lot of things."

Suggested reading: Fred Lockley, *Conversations With Pioneer Women* (Eugene: Rainy Day Press, 1981).

MOUNTAIN CHARLEY

Her name was probably Elsa Jane Forest, but we're not sure. She married a Mississippi River pilot. A few months later they had a son — two years after that, a daughter. Her idyllic marriage ended when a man named Jamieson, the mate on her husband's boat, shot him to death.

When the shock wore off, the widow, only fifteen, learned that she was penniless. She placed her children with the Sisters of Charity. Consumed with hatred for Jamieson, she dedicated her life to avenging her husband's death.

How best could she do that? How could a young woman track down a riverboat man if she knew nothing about him but his name? Elsa was tall and her facial features resembled a teen-aged boy. An asthmatic problem had left her voice hoarse.

"I'll become a man," she vowed. "That's how I'll find this Jamieson."

When she first started wearing men's clothing, she only ventured out at night, fearful of discovery. Within three weeks she was going anywhere and everywhere.

The Masonic lodge buried her husband and gave her seventy dollars. With that and her new disguise, she began her search. She found work as a cabin boy on a boat at thirty-five dollars a month.

After four years on the river, she had not found Jamieson, and she became a brakeman on the Illinois Central Railroad.

"I saw and heard much that was unsuitable for a woman," she wrote in her autobiography.

But how else could she send money regularly to the Sisters who were raising her children? Besides, Elsa thought that being a man in the strict Victorian society of the 1850s was better than being a woman.

She finally found Jamieson, gambling in a St. Louis saloon. She followed him outside and accosted him. She told him who she was as she drew her pistol. Perhaps she was nervous. She missed, and Jamieson shot her in the thigh. She fired again, hitting his arm as he ran away.

She lived as a women during her six-months' recovery. Then, in 1855, she reverted to her former life and became a bullwhacker in an emigrant party to California. The other emigrants thought she was an eighteen-year-old boy. They complimented her on her hunting skill.

While crossing the Black Rock Desert on the Lassen Cutoff, the emigrants came upon a woman and two children, who were all near death.

"My husband went ahead to find feed for the team," the woman

said, her weak voice barely audible. "The team died that same day, and we ain't had nothing to eat for four days. Don't know why he didn't come back."

The emigrants learned a few miles further, when they found his body.

"I longed to disclose to her my sex, and minister to her in that manner in which only one woman can to another," Elsa wrote. "Yet I did not dare to, and I was forced to give her only that rough consolation which befitted my assumed character."

Elsa tried mining. Then she got a job in a Sacramento saloon. Within six months she had become a partner in the business. She sold out and went into mule packing. Again she was successful, still posing as a man, of course. But she left her mule-train partner to run the business and returned to the states to see her children.

After a few months visiting as a woman, she returned to her disguise and headed back to California. This time she led an wagon train of fifteen men. She drove a large herd of cattle to sell in California.

Attacked by Shoshoni Indians along the Humboldt River, the train lost one man killed and had several wounded. Elsa stabbed one Indian and shot another, being wounded herself in the furious fight.

The packing business had flourished. Elsa ran it for a time and then sold out. Between that and her herd of cattle, she had thirty thousand dollars to send home.

St. Louis bored her, and she headed back west for some new adventure. It was 1859 and the young woman — now twenty-two and back in male disguise — joined the Pike's Peak Gold Rush. She had no luck. Other prospectors began calling her Mountain Charley.

She opened a saloon, married her bartender, and ran into Jamieson again while riding her mule to Denver. This time her draw was quicker and her aim better. She put three bullets in him, but he recovered only to move to New Orleans and die of yellow fever.

Charley and her husband returned to the states, and she had no more reason for the disguise. She was satisfied, after an adventurous thirteen years, to go back to being a woman.

Suggested reading: Mrs. E. J. Guerin, *Mountain Charley* (Norman: Univ. of Oklahoma Press, 1986).

A CONTENTED MIND AND SOMETHING TO EAT

Eleven-year-old Priscilla Merriman was taken out of school in her native Wales because of her mother's poor health. The girl had to care for younger brothers and sisters.

Five years later the mother died, and Priscilla became the woman of the house. The lonely girl heard about the Mormon religion at a neighborhood meeting. She joined the church at sixteen, over her father's objection.

Priscilla met Elder Thomas Evans at church. The youngest of eight children, Evans had lost his father at four. He went to work at seven, learning the trade of iron roller in a foundry. At nine, he lost a leg on the job.

Priscilla enjoyed hearing Thomas explain the Mormon gospel.

"He's congenial," she said. "He has a fine tenor voice and he speaks so nice."

Soon engaged, they married in April, 1856, just before Priscilla's twenty-first birthday. Two weeks after their marriage, they boarded ship in Liverpool, emigrating to Zion.

Priscilla, pregnant, was sick all the way across the ocean. They rode cattle cars from Boston to Iowa City, where they waited three weeks for their handcart. Thomas turned down ten dollars a day to stay in Iowa City and work in a foundry.

"We're anxious to get to Zion," he said. "Money doesn't mean that much."

They pushed their handcart a thousand miles to Salt Lake. Priscilla was sick and tired every night.

"What a glorious way to come to Zion," the indomitable woman said. Thomas agreed.

Priscilla and her one-legged husband shared a tent on the journey with eighteen others, including two blind men, a one-armed man, and a widow with five children.

One day an Indian visiting their camp admired Priscilla. Thomas, who liked a joke, said the Indian could have her for a pony. The next day the Indian returned with an extra horse, asking for his pretty little woman.

"I was never so scared," Priscilla said. "Our captain had to talk a blue streak to make the Indian see it as a joke."

They reached Salt Lake in early October. Greeted with prayers, hymns, and great exaltations, they were glad to get through the mountains so early. Later groups that year became snowbound in Wyoming, and many died.

Priscilla and Thomas went on to Spanish Fork, where they shared a one-room dugout with a family of four. They slept in a bed

for the first time since leaving the ship in Boston. On the last day of December, their daughter, Emma, was born. Priscilla made baby clothing from old underwear, discarded by a neighbor.

She and Thomas worked a year for two acres of land and began construction of a two-room adobe house. By then they had another daughter, Jennie.

Thomas made a large, springy bedstead of timber and rawhide. It came in handy when Caliline Louisa was born, as two of the children were then sleeping at the foot of their parents' bed. Priscilla made a mattress and pillows for the new bed from cattails gathered in a marsh.

In 1861 Priscilla had their first son, David. Thomas' parents came from Wales to live with them. The eight people crowded into their two rooms.

Thomas gave the adobe house to his parents, and he and Priscilla moved to town with their children. They lived in a one-room cabin while they built a new house. They bought a stove from a friend who was moving to California. Priscilla had never cooked on a stove before. She burned her first batch of bread.

In 1863 their second son, J. J., was born. Sarah, Charles, and Thomas followed at two-year intervals, but Thomas died at six months.

Thomas, senior, tried farming but was never good at it. After floods, grasshoppers, and crickets, he gave up and opened a store.

He had barely started in business when the church sent him on a mission to England. He mortgaged the new house to raise his travel money. Ada, their ninth child, came just after he left. By then he and Priscilla had a granddaughter. The two baby girls were raised as twins.

When Thomas returned from his mission, he sold their house to pay off the mortgage. His parents had died, returning the small house to Thomas and Priscilla.

Priscilla had twelve children in all. Her life's motto was to never look back — only forward.

"I always thanked the Lord for a contented mind, a home, and something to eat," she often said.

Suggested reading: Cathy Luchetti, *Women of the West* (St. George: Antelope Island Press, 1982).

IT WAS A NEW COUNTRY AND WE HAD A HARD TIME

Mary Ann Stucki was six when her Mormon parents emigrated from Switzerland to Utah. They walked the last thousand miles, traveling with a handcart battalion from Iowa City to Salt Lake City in 1860.

At first her parents pulled the cart, while Mary Ann and her brother pushed, and the two small ones rode. But the mother's feet swelled so she could not wear shoes. When the father had to hitch the family cow to the cart, Mary Ann's mother grew discouraged.

"Cheer up," Stucki said. "We're marching to Zion. The Lord will take care of us."

Mary Ann grew up at Santa Clara in the southwestern corner of the territory. At nineteen she married a man who already had a wife. When her husband died, Mary Ann had to marry again, as her parents were old and poor.

When John Hafen proposed, Mary Ann was reluctant to accept. John's first wife, Anna, did not want her husband to take another wife. Mary Ann cried for most of her wedding trip.

In 1891, after Mary Ann had borne six children, John moved her to a new settlement at Bunkerville, Nevada. Anna was already there, being helped by Mary Ann's son, Albert, sixteen. By that time, John had two more wives in Utah.

Mary Ann smiled when she saw Bunkerville, The young cottonwoods lining irrigation ditches seemed like an oasis in the desert. But when she saw her two-room shack with dirt floor and roof, she cried.

John returned to Santa Clara to serve as a bishop for the church.

"Albert," he said, "I'll leave you in charge of planting. Dig up some wild berry bushes and set them by the house. Someday they'll make shade from the blistering sun. Make it nice for your mother.

"Yes, pa."

That fall John returned from Utah with a wagon load of lumber. He and Albert built a floor and ceiling in Mary Ann's house and added a second story with a shingled roof. There was no inside stair, however; the children climbed to their rooms on an outside ladder. "I'm homesick, husband," Mary Ann said. "Could I go back with you for a short visit?"

John let her ride with him when he hauled back a load of grain to the grist mill. She broke down and cried at the familiar sights of her former home.

John's two Utah wives and his bishop duties kept him there most of the time. Mary Ann, now with a seventh child, had to rely on Albert to help raise the family.

John provided "a house, lot, and land and he furnished some supplies," she wrote. "But it was a new country and we had a hard time making a go of it."

They hauled their cotton sixty-five miles and exchanged it for cloth. Every year they put up twenty-gallon barrels of preserves.

Mary Ann's eighth and last child was born two years after the move to Bunkerville. Mary Ann had never been to a doctor in her life. John came to Bunkerville to see the new baby, a twelve-pound boy.

A year later Mary Ann's mother died. Mary Ann returned to Santa Clara for the funeral. She inherited seventy-five dollars, her share of money her mother had once received from relatives in Switzerland. Mary Ann's father was blind, but he still worked in the fields.

With her inheritance, Mary Ann bought store goods, hoping to resell them at a profit in Bunkerville.

"I did not want to be a burden on my husband," she said.

She picked cotton on shares, her baby on her back. But she had to give up the business of selling store goods. Profits were small, and goods sold on credit were seldom paid for, particularly when bought by Indians. In 1895, the year after her mother died, Mary Ann's oldest girl, seventeen-year-old Mary, got married.

The next year Mary Ann became a grandmother, and her eight-year-old boy died of measles. For years Mary Ann had wanted a kitchen and a cool cellar. Albert drove a team a hundred miles to the mountains, where he exchanged work in a sawmill for lumber.

John came over from Utah to help, and they built a nice cellar with a kitchen above. Albert had to make a second trip to the sawmill and exchange work for another load to finish the job. By that time, Mary's baby daughter had died, and Mary Ann was no longer a grandmother.

"Polygamy was hard on men as well as women," Mary Ann wrote. "We went into it in obedience to the Lord's command and strived to subdue our jealous feelings and live in accordance with the spirit of the gospel."

Suggested reading: Mary Ann Hafen, *Recollections of a Handcart Pioneer of 1860* (Denver: Privately printed, 1938).

NEELIE

"I'll do the cooking, mother," sixteen-year-old Cornelia Kerfoot said.

She had never cooked a meal, but neither had her mother. They always had servants in their Missouri home.

It was May 1, 1865, and Judge Kerfoot, his wife, nine children, and a nephew were dividing up the work for the journey to California. Younger sisters Henrietta and Emma would wash the dishes.

The emigrants elected Judge Kerfoot their captain. The train grew to sixteen wagons and ten families as it moved into Iowa and turned west.

Near Fort Kearney in early June, they joined others to make up a 45-wagon train. The army required emigrants to travel in trains of forty wagons or more in Indian country. By mid-June, the emigrants began seeing graves from trains ahead.

Neelie enjoyed meeting Sarah Raymond, one of the original group that had left Missouri together. Sarah kept a journal and wrote this about her friend:

"The first two or three weeks Neelie and her mother tried to learn to cook, and mother and I tried to teach them. It is no small undertaking to cook for a family of twelve; I do not blame Neelie for getting tired. She says they have such appetites it is not worth while to tempt them with extras.

"Neelie is the dearest, sweetest, most unselfish daughter and sister; it seems they all depend on her. The children go to her in their troubles and perplexities. Her father and mother rely on her, and she is always ready to do what she can for any and everybody that needs her help. She is unselfishness personified."

Neelie was also pretty. By the middle of June, Doctor Fletcher, the train physician, was coming around to ride beside her whenever duties permitted.

Neelie, Sarah, and other girls often rode their horses away from the train to pick flowers, climb hills, and enjoy themselves. One day the train had an Indian scare while the girls were away. Judge Kerfoot galloped after his daughter and chased her back, lashing her horse with his whip. Neelie laughed at the wild ride, but her father would not speak to her for a long time.

Sarah, a religious girl, beamed at Sunday worship on July 2, when Neelie led a long procession forward to enlist in the service of the Master. Neelie shook hands with the preachers and testified for Christ.

On July 18 eight young people, including Doctor Waid

Howard, another physician who also had his eye on Neelie, all climbed Elk Mountain, near the Medicine Bow River. Sarah, Neelie, and their friends enjoyed the flowers, the snow, and the scenery. By this time Sarah was writing in her journal about Doctor Fletcher's desperate love for Neelie.

The next day Neelie did not feel well. Three days later she got drenched in a cold rain. As she rode back to the train over frost-covered ground, she shivered uncontrollably.

"I feel weak, mother," Neelie said.

"You go to bed, then. I'll call Doctor Fletcher."

Sarah was shocked when she saw her friend that evening. Neelie had persuaded one of her sisters to powder and curl her hair and paint her pale face so she would not look bad for the doctor. Sarah said nothing to Neelie, but she scolded the sister.

"It's mountain fever," Doctor Fletcher said. "Sarah, will you stay with her? I'll ask Doctor Howard to help me, too."

Three days later, the wagon train divided. Part of it, including the Kerfoot wagon, continued west to California. The others, including the Raymond wagon, turned north to Montana.

Sarah wrote in her diary on the last day the train was together:

"Mr. Kerfoot's family and ours have been almost as one family since we have been on the road, and I have become greatly attached to all of them and especially to Neelie. They all love her so and depend on her for everything. She is a precious daughter, a darling sister, and a true friend."

Not until she reached Virginia City and got a letter from Neelie's cousin would Sarah know what had happened to her friend.

Neelie had died on August 1, four days after the wagon train divided. The two doctors worked all night, trying to save her. She died at early dawn.

One of the men found a large, flat stone and engraved Neelie's name, age, and date of death for a marker. After covering the grave with wildflowers, the saddened emigrants moved on toward California.

Suggested reading: Raymond and Mary Settle (eds.) *Overland Days to Montana in 1865* (Glendale: Arthur Clark Co., 1971).

CHINA POLLY

She traveled east instead of west, and she came as a slave, but she was a pioneer woman just the same.

Johnny Bemis fanned out his cards. He had four aces. Watchers of that 1871 saloon poker game in the mining camp at Warren, Idaho, sucked in their breath.

"Johnny's got the luck running tonight," someone said.

"I have no more to lose," the Chinese man said as Johnny raked in the dust from the center of the table.

"Stake the girl," Johnny growled.

The Chinese looked down at Johnny's gold and studied his weather-beaten face.

"You will put up all the gold?"

"This and more."

Johnny stood up and called the saloon-keeper. They went to the safe and Johnny brought back three more bags of dust. He pushed his gold to the center of the table, adding the three new bags.

Coarse breathing sounds from the watchers filled the stillness of the summer night.

"Stake the girl," Johnny repeated. His eyes gleamed like burnished silver, and his jaw muscles stood out in tight knots.

"This is more like it," someone whispered.

They had played all afternoon and into the night. Johnny had won and then lost and then won again, cleaning his opponent out.

The miners only knew the girl — the Chinese man's slave — as China Polly. She had been smuggled into San Francisco earlier that year and passed from tong leader to tong leader until she reached her purchaser in Warren. He had bought her sight unseen. Her beauty took the breath away. She was eighteen.

After a long moment, the Chinese man nodded. "Bring in the girl."

A young Chinese left the room and returned with Polly. She wore a tight yellow dress, slit to both knees. Her skin was clear olive, her eyes slightly almond-shaped. Someone remembered twenty years later that the breath sounds of the antagonists sounded like the exhaust of a steam engine.

"One hand," Johnny said. "Winner takes all."

The Chinese nodded.

Johnny shuffled the cards and slapped the deck down.

"Cut."

Johnny dealt. The Chinese stood pat.

"I'll be damned," came a voice from the crowd.

Johnny studied his hand, laid two cards down and drew two more.

The Chinese spread his hand face up.

"Three aces," someone gasped.

All eyes looked at Johnny, as he spread his hand out and leaned back — five clubs.

"Wal, don't that beat it all," someone said. Spectators pounded each other's backs as Johnny raked in the gold. The Chinese spoke softly to the girl, and she raised fear-filled eyes to Johnny's.

The crowd parted to let Johnny and Polly through. Johnny had a strut in his walk. Polly followed with mincing steps. No one paid attention to the two Chinese men as they walked out.

For several months Polly cooked for Johnny and washed his clothes, as he drifted from one mining camp to another. Then he returned to Warren and spent the day bucking the tiger in a faro game. Johnny won steadily until harsh words passed between him and the dealer. Johnny reached for his gun, but the gambler was faster. Johnny fell to the floor, a bullet in his chest.

Someone called for a doctor. But Polly, who had sat behind Johnny all day, took charge. She ordered him strapped to a horse, and she led the horse to their cabin. She nursed Johnny back to health. For many weeks it was touch and go.

When Johnny got well again, he knew he loved the girl, and he married her. When the mining ended, they disappeared.

Thirty years later a guide led an historian on a trip through central Idaho. A friendly old ferryman who said his name was Johnny Bemis helped them across Cripple Creek. He invited the men to stay the night. They met his wife, a tiny, smiling Chinese woman.

The historian returned several times to get the whole story of Johnny Bemis and his pioneer woman.

Johnny died twenty years later. Friends brought Polly to town to look after her, but she was unhappy there. She returned to the cabin she had shared for most of her fifty years with Johnny.

Suggested reading: James D. Horan, *Desperate Women* (New York: G. P. Putnam's Sons, 1952).

45

FIRST WOMAN ON PIKE'S PEAK

Reports of gold in Colorado reached eastern Kansas in early 1857. A gold-hunting party planned to leave Lawrence on May 23. Julia Archibald Holmes, young and pretty and a resident of Lawrence, hurried to Emporia to tell her husband, James, about the venture.

James, an ardent free-stater, had made several raids into Missouri. He had been arrested and was being taken back to Missouri for trial when he escaped and fled to Emporia. Julia knew where he was hiding.

"Can we go to Colorado, too?" she asked. "It sounds exciting. Better than being found and going back to Missouri for trial."

James agreed, perhaps as much for asylum as for excitement. They joined the party as it traveled west, bringing the total membership to forty-seven.

The group knew little about the route. By early July they could see Pike's Peak. On July 6 they camped at the entrance to the Garden of the Gods.

Some men left immediately to prospect for gold. Three, however, were more interested in the mountains. They climbed Pike's Peak. When they returned, their reports so excited Julia that she begged James into trying the climb.

"We can do it," she said, looking up at the peak. "It's so beautiful."

They set out on August 1. Julia's pack weighed seventeen pounds, James's thirty-five. Julia wore tight black pants, a hickory shirt, and moccasins. Between them they carried six quilts, a tin plate, a pail, a change of clothing, nineteen pounds of hardtack, a pound of sugar, a pound of pork, three-fourths of a pound of coffee, and a book of Emerson's poems.

They moved slowly through canyons and up steep, sometimes slippery, slopes. They reached timberline in three days, where they camped in a cave. They rested a day, while Julia wrote letters and James read Emerson.

At the first light of dawn, they broke camp and moved toward the summit. Tiny blue flowers, spread across the slopes, fascinated them.

"They're bewitchingly beautiful," Julia wrote, "the children of sky and snow." They reached the summit just after noon. Julia was the first woman to climb the 14,110-foot peak.

Julia and James tarried to enjoy the magnificent views. They looked east across flat plains, melting into the horizon, over a hundred miles away. To the west, across South Park, they marveled at the Continental Divide. Peaks reached to the clouds, puffs of white against a brilliant field of blue. Forgetting the cold, Julia read Emerson's poem, Friendship, aloud to her husband.

My careful heart was free again,
O friend, my bosom said,
Through thee alone the sky is arched,
Through thee the rose is red;

All things through thee take nobler form,
And look beyond the earth,
The mill-round of our fate appears,
A sun-path in thy worth.

Me too thy nobleness has taught
To master my despair;
The fountains of my hidden life
Are through thy friendship fair.

When she finished the poem, she wrote to a friend, saying, "Just being up here fills the mind with infinitude and sends the soul to God."

It began to snow, and Julia and James hurried back down to their camp at the Garden of the Gods. A few days later, no one having found gold, the party broke up. Some went north to Cherry Creek and continued prospecting. Others, including Julia and James, went south to winter at Taos.

When spring came Julia and James decided to stay in the new territory of New Mexico. James became territorial secretary and Julia the New Mexico correspondent for Horace Greeley's New York Tribune.

The bonds they strengthened on the top of the mountain did not last. James stayed in the West, but Julia went East to work for woman's suffrage. She became secretary of the National American Woman Suffrage Association in Washington, D. C. Later she became the first woman member of the United States Board of Education.

Suggested reading: David Dary, *True Tales of the Old-Time Plains* (New York: Crown Publishers, 1979).

JULIA ARCHIBALD HOLMES

Denver Public Library, Western History Dept.

48

JOSEPHINE MEEKER

Colorado Historical Society

49

MILITARY INQUIRY

"Did Persune treat you well?" asked General Charles Adams, Colorado Militia.

"I don't know what to say," Josephine answered. The tall, attractive, twenty-year-old blonde had graduated from Oberlin College in the spring of that 1878 year. Then she had joined her parents, Nathan and Arvella Meeker, at the Ute Indian Agency. Full of ideals and anxious to improve the Indians, she set up a school for Indian children.

Only three students came, and the parents of two of those pulled them out before the schoolhouse was completed. The Indians had nothing against Josephine, but they wanted to protest her father's policies about making them farmers. Plowing the soil violated their religious beliefs. The earth, their mother, should not be disturbed.

"They acted about as I expected when I was captured," Josephine continued. "I knew the Utes and their natures pretty well."

"This is an official investigation," Adams said. "You were a captive for three weeks. I need to hear the full truth. Nothing will go to the newspapers."

"We were insulted a good many times. We expected to be." Her mother and another woman, Mrs. Price, had also been captured.

"What did the insult consist of?"

"Outrageous treatment at night."

"Am I to understand that they outraged you several times at night?"

"Yes, sir."

"Forced you against your will?"

"Yes, sir."

"Did they threaten to kill you?"

"Persune did not — well, only once. I asked him one night if he wanted to kill me. He said he did, so I said to get up and shoot me, but just leave me alone. He just turned over and didn't say any more that night."

"Was it done while his own squaws were in the same tent?"

"Yes, sir."

"Did any others do the same thing?"

"No, sir; not to me. Persune took me as his squaw. Of course, the rest did not dare to come around."

"Did Chief Douglas ever offer you any insult?"

"Not to me, but he did to my mother. His squaws were

jealous. They did not want her in their tent."

The chief's son had been the last one in Josephine's school. He had withdrawn the child on September 28. Nathan Meeker, worried, sent a message to the nearest army post, 170 miles to the north. Indians killed the bearer twelve miles outside the agency.

The Indians attacked the agency the next afternoon. By five o'clock all the white men had been killed and the buildings set afire. The women tried to flee to safety.

Persune, one of the younger Utes, called out to Josephine: "Come to me; no shoot you."

Josephine had no choice. It was soon evident that Chief Douglas wanted Josephine for himself, but Persune refused to give her up.

General Adams, a thorough man, wanted all the details of the massacre. He wanted to punish the guilty Utes without implicating any innocent ones.

"Did you ever see your father's clothes in anyone's possession?" he continued.

"One Indian had father's shoes on. I forget what his name was. I knew him well enough."

"Did you see his coat?"

"No, but I saw his pants; I do not know who had them."

When General Adams asked the inevitable question of Mrs. Meeker, she replied:

"I was made clear to me that if I did not submit I would be killed. After I gave up, nothing more was said. I had connection once with Douglas. I was afraid he had disease."

Persune never got over his love for Josephine Meeker. He promised her that if she stayed with him, she would never have to work. He offered her all his possessions, and he cried when she went away with General Adams.

Josephine worked for a time in the Office of Indian Affairs in Washington. Then she became a secretary for one of Colorado's senators. She died quite young.

When the Utes heard of Josephine's death, they said Persune should paint his face black in mourning. No one knows if he did.

Suggested reading: M. Wilson Rankin, "The Meeker Massacre," in *Annals of Wyoming.* XVI (1944).

PICKLED HUSBAND

Virginia Dale moved in with Jack Slade when Slade worked in Wyoming for Russell, Majors & Waddell, the freighters, stagers, and operators of the Pony Express. Pretty and a crack shot, Virginia had enough spirit to keep up with her common law husband, who one day would be called the meanest man in the West.

When Big Ben Holladay bought out Russell, Majors & Waddell, he asked their toughest men to stay on and work for him. Slade, the toughest of the lot, became superintendent of the most dangerous division. That division extended from a station near the Wyoming border to Julesburg, Colorado. Slade made the border station his headquarters, naming it Virginia Dale after his mistress.

Virginia and Slade moved into the twenty by sixty-foot log headquarters building and set up housekeeping in the back rooms. A cellar corral below the building sheltered station livestock during Indian attacks.

Virginia cooked for the stock tenders and stage drivers and passengers. Slade was gone much of the time, chasing road agents, dishonest employees, and horse thieves out of his division. Virginia had no trouble running the station when Slade was gone.

"Slade cleaned up the worst division on the line," Holladay bragged. "I knew he was the toughest superintendent I could get. And that woman of his is just as tough. They make a good pair."

Virginia heard stories of the dozen new notches in Slade's pistol. She didn't ask questions about them. She also heard that Slade had hanged a few men that he did not shoot.

Slade was a hard drinker, and he began killing for plain meanness and not for company benefit. Finally Holladay had to fire him. Slade was drunk when Holladay rode up and strode into the station.

"You're through, Slade," Big Ben roared. "Get your gear and clear out."

Holliday watched Virginia carefully, more worried about her than her drunk husband. Slade drew his pistol, but he was slow. Holladay slapped the gun aside, keeping his own pistol on Virginia.

"Get off the station, both of you," Holliday ordered. "You're through working for me."

Virginia and Slade moved to Virginia City, Montana, which had even less law than Wyoming or Colorado. They tried ranching, and Slade also freighted supplies from Fort Benton to the Montana gold mines. He became friends with another freighter, Jim Kiscadden. But Slade kept drinking and began terrorizing Virginia City, as he had done earlier in Colorado.

One night Slade rented a room in town and went on a roaring drunk. The next morning the landlord complained to the vigilantes. They captured Slade and dragged him to a corral with a high pole above its gate.

The meanest man in the West, his reputation known from the Missouri River to the Pacific Ocean, cried and cringed in terror as the vigilantes slipped the noose over his head.

"My God, my God," he begged. "Must I die? Oh my poor wife."

He pleaded with the vigilantes to send for Virginia so he could tell her goodbye. Finally one of them rode away to get her.

Virginia whipped her horse to its fastest speed, but she arrived a few minutes late. The box had been kicked out from under her lover. She looked up in horror as Slade's body twisted slowly in the Montana sunshine.

"Some of you were his friends," she screamed. "Why didn't you shoot him so he wouldn't suffer? I would have done that much for him. No dog's death should have come to such a man as he was."

Wild with rage, Virginia continued to curse the vigilantes. She threatened to cut out Kiscadden's heart. He had helped with the hanging.

"My husband's body will never be polluted by the soil you bastards walk on," she swore.

Virginia hired a carpenter to build a zinc-lined coffin for her lover. She laid Slade's body out, filled the coffin with alcohol, and had it pushed under her bed.

"Hell, he was pickled all the time I knew him," she said. "Might as well keep him that way now. He'd probably like it."

Three weeks after the hanging, Virginia opened a grand ball in Virginia City by entering arm in arm with Jim Kiscadden, the man whose heart she had threatened to cut out. For the rest of the winter her bed springs creaked above the room's third occupant.

When spring came Virginia had Jack freighted to Salt Lake City and buried in an old Mormon cemetery. The grave of the man in the zinc-lined coffin is now a bizarre attraction for tourists.

Suggested reading: Ellis Lucia, *The Saga of Ben Holladay, Giant of the Old West* (New York: Hastings House, 1959).

FURY AT LOST RIVER

The Modoc Indians would not live on a reservation with their ancient enemies, the Klamaths. They refused to leave their homeland in the Lost River area along the Oregon-California border.

That area also looked good to white settlers, who moved in. Some of them clashed with the Modocs; others hired them as ranch hands.

The immigrants included a family from Australia, William Boddy, his wife, his two sons, and his wife's daughter and her husband, Nicholas Schira.

"Aye, we neither hate nor befriend the natives," Boddy said. "We're just thankful for a chance to make a living on the soil."

Like all settlers they thought the land belonged to them. Twenty years of trouble between the settlers and the Indians came to a head on November 28, 1872, when thirty-eight soldiers marched from Fort Klamath to Tule Lake. They arrived in early evening with orders to arrest Captain Jack, the Modoc leader.

The army hoped to bargain the return of Captain Jack for a tribal promise to move to the reservation, thus ending the white-Indian conflict.

The Modocs had camped along the Lost River, near several cabins of settlers. Dennis Crawley lived closest to the Modoc Camp.

"We'll make a surprise move just before daylight," the army commander told Crawley. "We'll have Captain Jack in our custody before his men can organize any resistance. That way, nobody will get hurt."

"Sounds good," Crawley said. "It's best to move fast so there'll be no shooting." He saw no need to warn the settlers farther away.

Earlier that day, settler Henry Miller, a friend of the Indians, assured them that he knew of no plans for soldiers to come so late in the year. He said he would tell them immediately if he heard anything different.

The night was bitter cold, and the soldiers slipped up on the Indian camp in a freezing rain. But all the Modocs were not in that camp. Another band, led by Hooker Jim, had camped across the river.

When gunfire sounded in Captain Jack's camp, Hooker Jim led his band to an attack on the settlers. That morning Boddy, Schira, and Boddy's oldest son were working in the woods. The younger son was herding sheep for the neighboring Brotherton brothers.

Mrs. Boddy looked out from her cabin and saw her husband's

mule team pulling a wagon home with no driver.

"My word," she said to herself. "Something must have happened to William and the others."

She caught the team and tied them and then called her daughter. The two women slipped quietly into the woods, fearful of what they would find. When they heard Indian yells retreating toward the Brotherton cabin, their hearts sank.

Schira's body, stripped and mutilated, was the first found. As her daughter shrieked in anguish, Mrs. Boddy went on to find the bodies of her husband and his son.

Other settlers found the bodies of the Brotherton brothers and Boddy's younger son. When the Indians left the Brotherton cabin, they had met Henry Miller, their friend who had promised to warn them if the soldiers were coming. The broken promise became Miller's death warrant.

When the bloody day ended, fourteen settlers, all men and boys, lay dead.

"We do not kill women," the Modocs boasted.

The Modocs surrendered the next June. The men were wearing uniforms taken from soldiers they had killed in intervening months. The Indian women were wearing clothing taken from the Lost River settlers who had been murdered in November.

Colonel Jefferson C. Davis, Civil War veteran, commanded the Department of the Columbia. He invited Mrs. Boddy and Mrs. Schira to look at the captured Indians and see if they could identify any of them.

"I know it'll be hard on you ladies," Davis said. "Just do the best you can."

When they confronted the Indians, Mrs. Boddy drew a concealed knife, screaming, "That's one of the killers! That's Hooker Jim." She lunged forward, trying to stab the Modoc leader.

Mrs. Schira recognized another Indian. She drew a hidden pistol and tied to shoot him. She could not make the weapon fire.

Colonel Davis disarmed the two women, getting cut as he twisted the knife from Mrs. Boddy's hands. Then he turned to the two women and read them the riot act.

"I understand how you feel," Davis concluded. "But what's the difference between what you tried to do and what the Indians did?"

The anguished women had no answer.

Suggested reading: William Thompson, *Reminiscences of a Pioneer* (San Francisco, 1912).

THE COURTING OF SOPHIE ALBERDING

Sophie Alberding was born in Petaluma, California, in 1862, one of five children. Orphaned when Sophie was eleven, the children went to Illinois to live with an aunt. Sophie returned west on a train. Yet, her courtship experiences were typical of other pioneers in a land of blunt men and few women.

When Sophie was nineteen her brother Fred invited her to come visit him. He worked on the New Mexico ranch of a close family friend, Captain Joseph C. Lea. Sophie, whose future looked bleak in rural Illinois, accepted. He probably didn't tell his sister, but Fred's real reason was to find Sophie a husband.

Fred met Sophie's train in Las Vegas. Five days later their buckboard reached Roswell. Fred explained that Roswell was already a town of four *chozas*. Sophie learned on arrival that three of them — the post office, the store, and the blacksmith shop — were mere dugouts. But the Leas lived in an adobe house.

Fred repeatedly admonished Sophie on the ride down: "Now, Sis, I hope you'll try to be nice to all the men. You will find them gentlemen, in spite of some ways peculiar to the cowboy."

Sophie, thinking she knew more on the subject than her brother, responded, "Of course, I'll be nice to them. Don't you think I'm usually nice to people?"

"Well, sure, but I don't want them to think you're stuck up. You'll get used to their ways after awhile."

Captain Lea, six feet four, threw his arms around his tiny guest. Sophie weighed less than a hundred pounds, and her blonde hair hung in two braids, almost touching the ground.

"Fred," Lea shouted, "when we send you on an errand, you sure do a good job."

Sophie shared a room with the captain's widowed sister, Auntie Calfee, and her children. When she went in to supper that first evening, Sophie met twenty stares from young cowboys. When Mrs. Lea introduced her, Sophie noticed that no one stood up, but each cowboy nodded bashfully.

"Boys," Mrs. Lea said, "if I run short of boarders, I'll have Miss Sophie sit on the upstairs gallery where all the boys can see her. That should fill up the dining room."

"Wal," a voice drawled from the crowd, "Mis' Lea, I'd like for you to mention among the girls hereabouts that I got two new sheepskins for my *calchon*. Any nice girl as wants, can sure put her shoes under my bed."

The boisterous laugh deepened Sophie's embarrassment.

"Don't mind," Fred whispered. "You'll get used to it."

The cowboys soon began calling Sophie the "nickel-plated lady." Worried, she asked Auntie what it meant.

"Why, bless your heart. It means the best of everything. A cowboy'll spend all his money for a nickel-plated six-shooter or to decorate his spurs or bridle that way. What makes you ask?"

"I just wondered." Sophie smiled.

"You already made one conquest, dearie."

"What do you mean?"

"Jake — the one with the snake-bit hand. He asked for that second helping at breakfast just so you'd cut the meat for him. I heard him say you was the daintiest little heifer he ever done see."

One cowboy wanted to buy Sophie a dress. She refused indignantly.

"Whoever heard of a young man buying dresses for a *respectable* young lady," she complained to Mrs. Lea.

"You shouldn't be so hard on him. I know that back in the states, girls don't accept candy, flowers, or books from any man, save an affianced husband. But here it's different. I told him you'd be glad to accept a handkerchief. I hope you'll do it."

When roundup ended, the Leas gave a dance. They moved the furniture out of the dining room and sprinkled the dirt floor to keep down the dust. Sophie had an abundance of partners.

"I don't think I ever saw dancing partners put so much physical activity into the performance as these cowboys," she told Auntie.

John Chisum gave Sophie a pair of bracelets in a velvet-lined box that he had ordered from St. Louis. She didn't hesitate to accept the gift from the 64-year-old cattleman, already famous in New Mexico.

In ten months at the Leas, Sophie turned down seven proposals. Then she met John William Poe, who, as a deputy sheriff, was the man most responsible for the killing of Billy the Kid. Pat Garrett, the sheriff, and Captain Lea both told Sophie they hoped she would marry Poe.

"He'll be our next sheriff and will be a big man in the territory some day," they said.

When Sophie looked up at the tall, broad-shouldered Poe, she knew "the conqueror of the citadel had arrived."   T h e y married at 5:00 one morning in early May, 1883. The time selected allowed Poe to get back to Lincoln in two days, where he had to testify in a murder trial.

Suggested reading: Sophie Poe, *Buckboard Days* (Albuquerque: Univ. of New Mexico Press, 1981).

THREE WISHES

Grace McCance was three in 1885, when her family homesteaded twelve miles from Cozad, Nebraska. Grace's mother and the three children moved into the one-room sod house built the previous fall by father Charles.

"I've got a job with the team all summer at two dollars a day," Charles announced, overjoyed to have his family together again.

They owned a milk cow and chickens by winter.

Three years later the family had too many cows to picket, so six-year-old Grace became their herder.

"It's nice being outdoors," she told her mother, "but watching cows is boring. Could I have some leftover scraps? I can quilt for my corncob dolls."

When sewing tired her, Grace liked to lay on her back and look up at the fleecy clouds.

I wish I could fly high enough to look down on the clouds from above, she thought. I wonder what the clouds look like to angels?

Grace was eight before she made her first trip to town with her father. By the time she was ten, Grace had five sisters. She continued to make quilts.

"You know what I wish?" she asked her mother.

"What's that, Grace?"

"That some day people from far away will come to look at my quilts and say I did a good job."

"Maybe they will. You do pretty needlework."

When the family moved to a larger farm near the district school, Grace started her formal education. Still the family herder, she watched the cows from early morning until the first recess and from the last recess until dark. She corralled them between recesses so she could attend class.

When Grace was eleven she made her third wish.

"I want to marry a cowboy," she whispered to the clouds.

Grace had never seen a cowboy, but her geography book had a picture of one. He sat on a horse, watching a large herd of cattle.

Grace daydreamed that one day such a cowboy would ride up on a fine horse, leading another with a sidesaddle. The daydreams contained no romance. Grace would glide across the prairie to meet her chosen, step gracefully into the sidesaddle and ride away to herd cattle in style.

When Grace was eighteen the family — by then seven girls

and one boy — moved to a ranch on the open frontier of northwestern Nebraska. Grace missed the social life of her school and church.

But one day, when Grace's father was sick, a tall, handsome cowboy rode up.

"Name's Bert Snyder," he said. "Hear your pa's sick. I came to help out."

Grace lived in a dream world for the next few days. Will I ever see him again? she wondered as he rode away.

Grace studied hard in her new school to make up for the years as family herder. The next summer she took an eight-week course in North Platte, passed the county examinations, and got a certificate to teach third grade.

Her first school, in an isolated area sixty miles from home, had two pupils for Grace. After all the years in a large, lively family, Grace relied on her quilting to ward off the loneliness of the small school and the ranch where she boarded.

Another summer term brought a position in a larger school near her family. Then Bert Snyder came again to call. One day — just like her dreams — Bert rode up, leading a horse with a sidesaddle. He and Grace married when she was twenty-one.

The Snyders bought their first automobile in 1912, long before they had roads. When Ford started using gearshifts, Bert went back to horseback, leaving the driving to Grace. She drove her husband to distant windmills, gates, and fences needing repair. While he worked, she quilted. Her quilts became famous. One contained over ninety thousand pieces.

The Snyders' son married and built his house on the ranch. When the son's son became six, the closest school was twelve miles away. Roads were still bad, so Grace's son bought a small airplane and flew the boy to school and back each day. Grandma Grace loved to go along. When there was time, her son would fly high over the clouds and her last wish came true.

Eventually Grace's quilts, world famous, were exhibited from coast to coast. The insurance company would not allow them to be shipped as airline baggage. It always bought two tickets for each show, so Grace could take the window seat with the quilts on the seat beside. Grace would smile as she looked out the window, thinking of her three wishes.

Suggested reading: Nellie Snyder Yost, "Three Wishes", in *The Women Who Made the West* (New York: Avon Books, 1980).

PARADISE IN THE DESERT

When the Southern Pacific train pulled into Sentinel, Arizona Territory, that late August morning in 1888, Sadie Martin thought it the most desolate town she had ever seen. She hardly recognized John, brown as an Indian. Five months before, and married less than a year, he had left her back in Iowa to go west to help his father and brother build an irrigation canal in the Gila River bottom. His height and his smile told Sadie it was really he.

"Hot," Sadie said, throwing her arms around John.

"Wait 'till the sun's higher, darling. Your long sleeves will help. We've got an all day wagon ride to our claim."

The three Martin men had all filed homestead claims in the area to be irrigated. They lived there in tents with five Indian helpers. They worked on a large log cabin in the hours they could spare from supervising the canal construction.

"It will be a paradise in the desert," John had written, asking Sadie if she wanted to join them when the house was ready.

Sadie didn't want to wait. She came out immediately, not heeding John's warning about primitive living conditions.

When they reached the tents that evening, John's parents had to be careful greeting Sadie. Her face looked like a boiled lobster, and three rows of blisters ran down each arm, repeating the lace pattern in her sleeves.

Three days later Sadie saw her first sandstorm. They had just cooked a large dinner with freshly killed beef from a friendly neighbor when someone shouted, "Sand storm."

They threw aprons and dish towels over the food, and rushed it into a tent. But the food was too sandy for any of them to eat. They gave it to the Indians, who ate it, sand and all.

Building of the canal stopped for a time while John's father sued the company. He won the suit, and a new company was formed to continue construction. In the meantime the three men fenced and improved their claims, getting them ready for water. They planted potatoes in the low ground near the river. Sadie remembered that one of their favorite recreations was walking down on Sundays to hoe the potatoes and admire their growth.

Too far from Yuma for regular church services, they listened to a wandering preacher three or four times a year.

"But what a sermon it would be," Sadie wrote. "It was good to be reminded of our shortcomings, but sometimes we had the feeling that the preacher thought we were more wicked than we actually were."

The loneliness of the desert was so intense that dogs, horses,

60

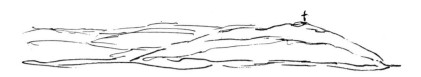

and even chickens took on personalities. Encountering another human was a real adventure.

Sadie and John's mother were proud of their chickens. They gave them names to suit their personalities. Sadie remembered a black one named Molly that tiptoed across the living room to lay her eggs in the bedroom. She would tiptoe out of the house before beginning her cackle.

Rattlesnakes were Sadie's biggest worry at first. Finally, she became quite expert at killing them. She tried to never let one get away.

A son, Brayton, came to bless Sadie and John in November, 1889. The baby became the center of the whole family's universe. When he cut his lip in a fall, his grandfather sewed it up with four stitches.

In February, 1892, the Walnut Creek dam failed and the rampaging Gila washed the Martin farms away.

"If it hadn't been for Brayton in those trying days, I do not know what we would have done," Sadie wrote. "He was growing dearer each day."

But three months later the boy died after a short, mysterious illness.

"We had a few wildflowers," Sadie said, "and father read the burial service. It seemed that our one bright star had set."

In October, 1893, Gladys was born. Sadie almost died from chills and fever afterward. As the baby grew, the anguish of losing Brayton gradually lessened.

Sadie went to Los Angeles for the birth of the second daughter, Marcella, who came on New Year's Day, 1895. They traded their ranch in 1897 for a house in Los Angeles.

Years later, after John had died, Sadie went back to look for the old, familiar places. She found the knoll where they had buried Brayton, but could not find the grave. When she reached the location of their ranch, she felt bitter disappointment.

"Not a tree, a fence post, or even the ruins of either house could be seen anywhere," she wrote. "Search as I did, I could see nothing but desert."

Suggested reading: Sadie Martin, "My Desert Memories," (Arizona Historical Society Library, Tucson, 1939).

ORDERING INFORMATION

True Tales of the Old West
is projected for 38 volumes.

For Titles in Print,
Ask at your bookstore
or write:

PIONEER PRESS
P. O. Box 216
Carson City, NV 89702-0216
Voice Phone (775) 888-9867
FAX (775) 888-0908

Other titles in progress include:

Frontier Artists
Army Women
Western Duelists
Government Leaders
Early Lumbermen
Frontier Militiamen
Frontier Teachers

Ghosts & Mysteries
Californios
Doctors & Healers
Homesteaders
Old West Merchants
Scientists & Engineers
Visitors to the Frontier